www.enchantedlion.com

First Reprint Edition published in 2018 by Enchanted Lion Books,
67 West Street, 317A, Brooklyn, New York 11222
Copyright © 1968 by Helen Borten
Copyright © 2018 by Enchanted Lion Books for reprint edition
Originally published in 1968 by Knopf, New York
Production and restoration: Marc Drumwright
All rights reserved under International and Pan-American Copyright Conventions.
A CIP record is on file with the Library of Congress

ISBN: 978-1-59270-230-5
1 3 5 7 9 8 6 4 2

Printed in China by RR Donnelley Asia Printing Solutions Ltd.
First Printing

HELEN BORTEN
THE JUNGLE

ENCHANTED LION BOOKS
NEW YORK

To Marvin

In a hot land near the equator, where winter never comes,
a new day is beginning. The climbing sun looks close enough
to touch as it turns the sky pink. Out of the mist a vast ocean
of leaves appears, splashed with yellow, orange, and violet
blossoms. It is the roof of the jungle. Butterflies dip in and
out of the blossoms. Macaws and parakeets feed and squawk
in the treetops. They drop more berries than they eat.
A vulture circles around and around overhead.

Here and there, tall trees poke up through the sea of green like watchtowers.
A spider monkey sits high in a tree munching fruit. Suddenly, a shadow
darkens its leafy perch as a hungry eagle drops from the sky. But the little
acrobat leaps away just in time. Leaves swish and close like waves behind
all the little monkeys as they disappear into the thick foliage.
The eagle will have to find its breakfast elsewhere.

Under the leafy roof, it is dim and still. Time seems to have stopped in a wild summer world of long, long ago. Thick vines hang from trees like ropes.

They twist around trunks and loop from branch to branch
in their journey towards the sun. The forest looks as if
it is tangled in an enormous net.

The trees are heavy with ferns and orchids and drooping
beards of moss. These are "air" plants trying to reach
sunlight by making their homes high above the ground.
Their roots take hold on bark instead of in the earth.
Dust collects around the roots, forming soil in which to grow.
There are air plants cupped like pitchers to store rainwater
and others with long roots dangling to the ground.

The jungle seems deserted.
But thousands of tricksters
hide behind the screen of leaves.
A piece of bark falls...
and becomes a lizard.
A leaf trembles...
and becomes a grasshopper.
A shaggy ball of moss unravels...
and becomes a sloth.
A vine uncoils...
and becomes a snake.
A spot of sunlight blinks...
and becomes a jaguar's eye.

Far below the tree dwellers, on the jungle floor, parasol ants
are on their way home carrying pieces of leaves bigger than
themselves. A spider spins its silk around a dozing wasp
that it will eat for lunch. Termites, ticks, land snails, scorpions,
mites, earthworms, and insects that have never been named
devour bits of dead wood, leaves, and insects that litter the ground.
Under the carpet of leaves, nuts and seeds that may someday
become giant trees begin to sprout in the damp clay soil.
Moths and beetles hide here, too, waiting for dusk. Only then
will they venture out and lift their wings.

From the ground, you cannot see the sky or feel the sun
or hear the wind. It is cool and silent in the twilight gloom.
Pale trunks disappear into the shadows above, like ghosts
trailing robes of green. There are no low branches anywhere.
Some trunks are covered with spikes. Some are smooth and
look to be carved out of bone. And some have so many air
plants molded around their bark that they will be strangled
to death. There are more different kinds of trees in the jungle
than anywhere else on earth.

High in the sky, the midday sun slips behind the clouds.
A crack of thunder splits the air. Rain crashes down
on the jungle's vast umbrella of leaves.
Small animals scurry into holes and crevices for shelter.
The rain seeps through the leaves and pours down in sheets.
It will rain everyday like this for a month or two.
Then, as suddenly as it began, the rain will stop.
The leaves will drip all through the night. Air plants shaped
like pitchers now hold enough water to drink for weeks to come.
The sloth shakes its fur. A frog leaps back onto its leaf,
no longer afraid of losing its grip. The cool air is filled
with the fragrance of flowers and spicy plants.

Sunlight blazes through a gap in the leaves left
by an uprooted tree. The fallen tree makes a handy
bridge for creatures not fond of getting their feet wet.
A cloud of dragonflies dances above the water,
their wings shimmering in the sun's rays. Giant leaves
form brilliant patterns in green, gold, and copper.
Slender bamboo poles shoot twenty feet high.
In this bright space, plants cram every inch,
as though celebrating their escape from the shade.

A crocodile slides out of the stream.
It stays so still as it suns itself
that it looks like a gnarled log.

The sky reddens; the leaves darken and grow more distinct as the sun slips behind the forest. An ear-splitting cry breaks the silence. The howler monkey, noisiest animal of all, is exercising his lungs. The air begins to hum with sounds like needles clicking and wheels whirring and brooms swishing. The insect orchestra is tuning up. Cicadas shrill, katydids fiddle, and crickets grind their scissors. From all directions voices join in the din. Mosquitoes buzz, frogs croak, woodpeckers tap, and toucans call hoarsely to each other.

Clouds of fireflies glimmer in the gathering darkness.
The jaguar slips from its den. The bat glides forth on leathery wings.
The horned owl opens its great ringed eyes.
This is the hour when many hunters come out to seek their prey.

As night falls, other animals venture out to feed.
An armadillo lumbers after ants. A deer laps gently
at a pool of rainwater. Opossums and porcupines
scuttle through the trees. Mice, lizards, and tortoises
rustle underfoot. A band of peccary, a kind of wild pig,
snort and dig their snouts into the soil, searching for food.
They leave in a noisy rush, but their musky odor lingers
in the air. Just before dawn, the bat hurries to find
its cranny, the owl its tree hole, the mouse its burrow.
The jaguar, its jaws still red, drags the rest of its kill home.
Moths and fireflies disappear under the leaves.
Worms draw back into the soil.

High in the trees, the birds are about to begin their morning chorus. On the branches, monkeys sit motionless, their long tails hanging down behind them, like dark quarter notes dotting the gray dawn. Soon the sun will chase the mist and another day will begin in the mysterious green world below.